KidLit-O Presents

What's So Great About Walt Disney?

A Biography of Walt Disney Just For Kids!

Blake Bibbins

KidLit-O Books

www.kidlito.com

Table of Contents

About KidCaps

KidLit-O is an imprint of BookCaps™ that is just for kids! Each month BookCaps will be releasing several books in this exciting imprint. Visit are website or like us on Facebook to see more!

To add your name to our mailing list, visit this link: http://www.kidlito.com/mailing-list.html

[1] Image: http://christmas-specials.wikia.com/wiki/Walt_Disney

Chapter 1: Introduction

Walt Disney wiped his forehead to keep the fat drops of sweat from rolling down into his eyes. Lifting his hand to block out the sun, he smiled at the sight of thousands of people walking down the crowded main street towards a giant castle – a castle that *he* had built.

Children were barely held back by their parents, some of them managing to run ahead, and the music played by the live band created a feeling of electric excitement in the air. All of the people streaming by Walt, stretching back as far as his eyes could see, were guests on the opening day of the park that he had personally designed and brought to life – Disneyland.

But as he watched those happy people, Walt became aware of a big problem - things weren't going as planned.

For one, the weather on this summer day, Sunday, July 17, 1955, was much hotter than he and his team had been expecting. It was only 10 AM and already everyone in the park was sweating. Of course, it didn't help that there were so many people bumping into each other everywhere they went. Refreshment stands were quickly running out of food and drinks, which was upsetting some guests.

As if that wasn't enough, there were way too many people in the park. Instead of the 6,000 or so special invitees that he had been expecting, Walt saw that almost 30,000 people were passing through the main gates. It appeared that someone had made illegal copies of the few real invitations and had sold them to the general public.

The reporters that Walt had invited to see his new theme park were not impressed so far with what they saw of Disneyland.

As if the high attendance and record heat weren't enough, things started to get even worse. Because Walt Disney wanted to make sure that his park opened on time, there had been a lot of details that were finished at the last minute. One of these had been the plumbing for the park's many water fountains and the finishing coat of asphalt covering the streets. But the fresh asphalt was still soft, and the heels of many ladies' shoes were sinking down into it. And because there was a plumber's strike going on in Anaheim, many of the water fountains still weren't working by the time the park opened.

In fact, some guests though that Disneyland was trying to force them to buy soft drinks from Pepsi, a major sponsor of the park. To top it all off, the news crews covering the park's grand opening decided to lay their camera wires across roads and sidewalks, tripping some of the guests.

Walt had worked so hard to make sure that this day would be unique and memorable – but he was quickly learning how unpredictable crowds of people can be. Unlike a small team working together at a movie studio, large crowds have a mind of their own and can do some pretty strange things. He would have to remember that in the future as he expanded his park and added new attractions.

Even though there were some unexpected problems that first day, Walt still felt immensely happy. He saw children laughing and running to hug their favorite cartoon characters. He saw families smiling together on adventure rides that took them to the jungles of Africa and India. He saw teenagers going to the moon on a rocket and saw older folks reminiscing happily as they thought about the small towns and main streets of their youth.

Walt had created Disneyland to bring people together and to inspire them. There were problems on its opening day, of course. And Walt and his team would fix those problems as soon as they could. But so far, it looked like the general public was just as excited about his park as he was.

Before long, the moment came for Walt Disney to talk to the world about his new park. Standing before the cameras, in front of the entrance to Disneyland, Walt knew that he could have said anything. But instead of taking the opportunity to pat himself on the back or to talk about how smart of a guy he was, Walt decided to just say a few sentences about what he hoped the new theme park would come to mean for young and old guests alike. After taking a deep breath, he smiled and said:

> "To all who come to this happy place - welcome. Disneyland is your land. Here, age relives fond memories of the past and here youth may savor the challenge and promise of the future. Disneyland is

dedicated to the ideals, the dreams, and the hard facts that have created America... with the hope that it will be a source of joy and inspiration to all the world. Thank you."[2]

With those few words, Walt Disney summed up his purpose for building the park, and really, his entire career. Everything that Walt Disney did - from sketching neighborhood pets as a child to making cartoons and building theme parks as a man – was meant to inspire his audience. Walt Disney wanted people to use their imaginations, just as he had been doing his entire life.

Today, the name Walt Disney is known the world over, and everyone from kids to adults knows him for the movies he made and for the parks he designed. But Walt Disney was not always celebrated for his talent and ideas. In fact, there were times when the people around him, both

[2]   Quotation:
http://history1900s.about.com/od/1950s/qt/disneyland.htm

family and business partners, thought that Walt Disney couldn't possibly make all of his dreams come true.

But even in his darkest moments, Walt Disney used his limitless imagination to picture how things could be. He used his mind to imagine entire worlds that didn't yet exist. He imagined ways of using new technologies to make animation more captivating and emotional. He imagined a life spent doing what he loved and making the world a happier place.

Walt Disney was the man behind Mickey Mouse, Donald Duck, and Goofy. He was also the man that brought the world live action movies and TV shows like *Swiss Family Robinson*, *Treasure Island*, and *Davy Crockett*. He created a company that keeps on entertaining children and adults alike almost fifty years after his death.

Walt Disney was a man who had both an incredible artistic talent and a powerful imagination.

His career as an artist began when he was just seven years old, living with his family in Marceline, Missouri.

Chapter 2: The Beginnings of Walt Disney's Imagination

3

---
[3] Image: https://d23.com/walt-disney-archives/about-walt-disney/

Walter Elias Disney was born on December 5, 1901, in Chicago, Illinois. His parents, Elias and Flora Disney, were extremely kind people who raised their large family (four sons and one daughter) they best that they could. Walt and his family lived in several different houses in several different cities over the years, moving wherever his parents could find work. His father Elias, before he got married to Walt's mother, had even moved from Canada to California to see if he could find any gold there. After having some pretty bad luck in his gold hunt, Elias eventually settled down to farm and to start a family.

Walt Disney's great-grandfather had also made a similar big move – from Ireland to Canada. The Disney family had originally moved from northwest France to Britain way back in the year 1066. Their name in France was spelled "d'Isigny" and meant "someone from the village of Isigny". But once the family arrived in at their new English-speaking country, the spelling was changed to "Disney".

Walt Disney was a busy child. Growing up in a safe home with plenty of spare time, it wasn't long before he discovered his artistic abilities. In particular, he found that he liked drawing the animals that he saw in the neighborhood.

When Walt was about five years old, he and his family moved to the city of Marceline, in Missouri. Although they only spent about four years in that small town, growing up there would make a powerful impression on young Walt's personality. The sights and sounds that surrounded him each day became a part of his character, and would pop up from time to time in different projects that he worked on.

For example, Marceline's main street would become the model he used for Main Street, USA in Disneyland, and the town itself would serve as the inspiration for the small town used in the film *Lady and the Tramp*.

When he was still a young boy, Walt decided to try and find a job to make a little money. He found work as a newsboy, selling papers and snacks to the passengers that came through on the Atchison, Topeka and Santa Fe Railway train. These were happy days spent seeing people from all across the country stopping over on their way to important meetings and trips.

Walt Disney is the boy in the center of this photo, on the right. The photo is from a meeting of newsboys[4]

When Walt was growing up, Marceline, Missouri, was a town that depended on the trains constantly stopping there. Working as a newsboy at the station, Walt was constantly surrounded by big trains carrying valuable cargo and people. He loved the sounds that the trains made and the way the ground rumbled as they rolled across the tracks. He loved the train horns and the smell of the engines. He loved the hustle and bustle of a busy train station.

All of this train culture had a profound effect on young Walt, and it wasn't long before he found himself obsessed with everything about trains. Through the years, he often included them in his cartoons and movies. In fact, when he had enough money later on, he even built a small steam train in the backyard of his home and took his daughters and their friends around on rides. He called the train the "Lilly Belle" (after his wife) and said that it was part of the "Carolwood Pacific Railroad".

Walt had so much fun taking houseguests around on his home train set that, when he designed Disneyland years later, he made sure to include a train that circled the entire park.

Walt's uncle was a train engineer that often passed through the station the Walt worked at. When he knew that his uncle would be coming through, young Walt would often get down on his knees and put his ear to the rails to see if he could hear a train coming. Whenever one passed by, Walt would try and spot his uncle and wave to him as the train passed through the station.

By the time he was about seven years old, Walt started to spend more time with one of his family's neighbors, a retired doctor named Doc Sherwood. Doc had a beautiful horse named Rupert that Walt enjoyed drawing pictures of.

Seeing an opportunity to help out a kid to develop his talent, Doc began buying the drawings that young Walt made of Rupert. Walt was thrilled. Imagine, someone giving him money to do something that he loved to do!

A few years later, when his family moved to Kansas City, Walt kept working hard to develop his talent by attending Sunday art classes. Moving to Kansas City was an important turning point for young Walt. Not only did he get a chance to learn more about drawing and art from real professionals, but he was also introduced to the world of theaters, moving pictures, and theme parks.

While going to school at Benton Grammar School, Walt met a fellow student (also named Walter) whose family genuinely liked to go to the theater and to watch movies (something that was still pretty new back in 1911). Young Walt Disney began spending more and more time with his friend Walter and truly grew to love the idea of entertaining people. He loved to see the joy and excitement that audiences felt when they went to the theater, and it wasn't long before Walt decided that he wanted to be a part of that world.

Kansas City also showed Walt the wonder of theme parks. Walt used to take his kid sister Ruth to stand outside the gate of a place called the Electric Park, which had rides and games. Too poor to buy tickets to go in, the two kids would look into Electric Park and imagine what it would be like to be inside. Each night, the park had a fireworks display, something that Walt would later use at Disneyland.

As much as he loved the excitement and entertainment of a theme park, there was one thing that Walt didn't like about Electric Park: was how dirty it was. He wanted to build a theme park of his own, but he would make sure that his was clean.

In 1917, when Walt was 16, his family moved back to his hometown of Chicago. Walt, convinced now that he wanted to make a living with his artistic talents, took night courses at the Chicago Art Institute and began to work as a cartoonist for his school newspaper. He drew political cartoons in the newspaper, and not long after dropped out of high school altogether to join the army.

World War One was raging, so Walt felt that it was his duty to help his country and its allies to win the war. But at 16 years old, Walt was too young to fight and the army rejected him. So Walt decided to try something different: he and a friend lied about their ages and signed up to be ambulance drivers for the Red Cross in France. Soon after the war in Europe ended, Walt got on a boat and sailed to France to drive an ambulance and to help Europe rebuild after the war.

Instead of camouflage or normal army colors, Walt's ambulance was decorated with cartoons faces.

When Walt came back to the United States after one year of being an ambulance driver, he had trouble finding work as a cartoonist. So his brother Roy (who was working at a local bank) used a business connection to get Walt a job working at an ad agency named the Pesmen-Rubin Art Studio. While there, Walt drew

[5] Image: http://en.wikipedia.org/wiki/File:Walt01.jpg

advertisements for newspapers, magazines, and movie theaters.

While at that studio, Walt met a very talented artist named Ubbe Iwerks, and the two decided to start an art company together, doing mainly the same type of work that they had been doing. Called "Iwerks-Disney Commercial Artists", the company was a great idea, but didn't end up lasting too long because there weren't enough clients.

It wasn't long before both Disney and Iwerks had to go and look for work elsewhere. They both found work at the Kansas City Film Ad Company, where they made animations for television advertisements.

At the Kansas City Film Ad Company, Walt and Ubbe worked with cutout animation, which is where pieces of paper are cut into different shapes and laid out on a table. The shapes may look like people, cars, planes, or anything else that the animator can think of. In order to create the feeling of movement, the animator takes a picture of the shapes, moves them slightly, and takes another picture, and so on. When all the pictures are shown one right after the other, it looks like they are alive and moving on their own.

Cutout animation was fascinating, but the artist inside Walt wanted to see what other kinds of animation were out there. He started doing some research to satisfy his curiosity. One day, he came across a book called *Animated Cartoons: How They Are Made, Their Origin and Development*, written by a man named Edwin G. Lutz. The book mentioned something that Walt knew remarkably little about - "cel" animation.

Instead of using pieces of paper to create the appearance of movement, cel animation uses drawings made on transparent sheets of a plastic-like material. To make a cartoon using cel animation, the artist draws many images on many different sheets of plastic and then takes a picture of each one on top of a moving background. Then, when all the drawings are seen in a row, it looks like a moving drawing.

Walt liked cel animation because it let him put his drawing talents to work. He thought that cel animation had a more promising future than cutout animation, so when Walt's boss saw how excited Walt was about this different way of animating, he let him borrow a camera to experiment with at home. It wasn't long before Walt was making projects of his own using this exciting technique.

The "American Dream" is usually described as a person who, if they work hard enough and believe enough in what they are doing, can accomplish anything. Walt Disney was born into an average American family, but he developed his talents enough to be able to earn a living doing what he loved most – drawing.

It was around this time (1919) that Walt Disney really put his imagination to work for him. He began to look at his life and career and imagine what could be. He looked at cel animation technology and pictured the amazing stories that he could tell and how he could entertain large audiences.

By 1919, Walt Disney had decided what he wanted to do with his life - he would entertain people with cartoon animations.

Chapter 3: Walt Disney's Career

Using the cel animation technique that he recently discovered, Walt and a fellow artist soon started up another company, making short films they called Laugh-O-Grams. The Laugh-O-Grams made fun of news and life in the Kansas City area, and people loved his short films and animations. In fact, Walt made enough money to hire several additional animators to make more short films.

He even started to develop another series of films called "The Alice Comedies", which would use both live actors and animations, but his studio soon ran out of money. With just a few dollars to his name, Walt decided to get a fresh start out in Hollywood, California with his brother Roy.

The company that Roy and Walt formed in 1923 was called "Disney Brothers' Cartoon Studio", and focused on making short films. "The Alice Comedies" series starred different young actresses who interacted on screen with various animated characters, talking and playing with them.

Walt and Roy soon found that they had too much work on their hands filming the actors, drawing and photographing the animations, and editing the final piece together. So the two Disney brothers hired some more artists to work in their studio, one of which was a young woman named Lillian Bounds. She started work as an ink artist, coloring in the drawings made by the animators, but within a few months she was offered a new position – as Walt Disney's wife!

With things going well both at home and at work, Walt Disney was happy with his life in California.

"The Alice Comedies" films were distributed by a woman in New York City named Margaret Winkler and later by her husband Charles Mintz. Charles Mintz taught Walt Disney the value of quality work by setting extremely high standards for "The Alice Comedies" film series.

But soon after Charles Mintz took over, Walt Disney learned that quality was not the only thing that mattered when it came to creating animations –money also mattered. For people like Charles Mintz, the most notable thing on his mind was the amount of money that each film cost to make.

While Mintz wanted to entertain audiences like Walt did, he also wanted to make sure that his company made a lot of money. So in 1927, Mintz asked Disney (and animator Ubbe Iwerks, who had previously moved out to Hollywood to work with Walt) to create a new animated character that could be used in cartoon shorts. Mintz felt that cartoon shorts would cost less money to make than "The Alice Comedies", which were mixed live action and cartoon films.

So Walt and Ubbe sat down to create a new character. They wanted to create a character that could make both kids and adults laugh out loud and want to come back for more. After lots of hard work, in September of 1927 they came up with Oswald the Lucky Rabbit. Audiences everywhere fell in love with Oswald and his silly antics.

[6] Image: http://www.youtube.com/watch?v=N21I6sIASiU

Oswald the Lucky Rabbit had lots of personality. He liked to go on adventures and was immensely brave. He even had a terrific sense of humor and used his body in all sorts of strange ways. For example, it wouldn't be strange to see Oswald twist himself up like a tornado, only to spin back the other way.

Although his cartoons were silent, Oswald quickly became the one of the most popular cartoons in the country – almost as popular as Felix the Cat. By the spring of 1928, Walt knew that his cartoon was making him terribly famous (and was making Charles Mintz and his company very rich). So in February of 1928, Walt Disney flew out to New York City to see if Mintz would pay him a little more money for each Oswald cartoon short. After all, Walt wanted to be able to give his animators more money for the high quality work that they had been doing.

But when Walt arrived in New York to speak with Mintz, he got the surprise of a lifetime: Mintz wanted to pay Walt *less* money for his and his team's time and effort. Walt was shocked! He knew that Mintz was more focused on the business side of things, but he couldn't imagine producing high quality Oswald cartoons for any less money than he was currently making.

When the two men couldn't come to an agreement, Charlie Mintz decided that the best solution would be to just take away the rights to Oswald the Lucky Rabbit. He also stole away most of Walt's animation team so that Mintz's company could keep making more Oswald cartoons.

After just one business meeting, Walt Disney went from sitting on top of the world to being left with almost nothing.

One animator stayed with Walt – his loyal friend Ubbe Iwerks. Ubbe and Walt knew that they were in trouble. They didn't have enough money to make the expensive *Alice Comedies* anymore, and they weren't allowed to make any more Oswald cartoons.

They needed to come up with a new character that would help their studio to make some money. But they couldn't come up with just any character – they needed someone that the world could fall in love with. They needed a character that would be funny, lovable and mischievous all at the same time.

What they came up with was this:

---
[7] Image: http://tinyurl.com/8ywxzgb

Walt drew the original idea for someone he called "Mortimer Mouse". The character was based on a pet mouse that he had adopted while working in one of his short-lived studios back in Kansas City. Ubbe made some artistic changes to make the mouse easier to draw when animating, and then Walt showed his wife the new character.

His wife Lillian liked the mouse, but she didn't like the name. She thought "Mortimer" didn't sound terribly appealing, and suggested that Walt name him "Mickey Mouse" instead. Walt agreed.

Walt and Ubbe made two cartoons featuring Mickey, but no one was tremendously interested in distributing them. The cartoons were silent and black and white, and no one thought that they were too special.

Frustrated that no one was interested in his new character Mickey Mouse, in the summer of 1928 Walt and Ubbe decided to try something new – making a cartoon with sound. Although other studios had tried making cartoons with sound, it never quite worked out.

But in 1927, a motion picture called *The Jazz Singer* used synchronized sound that matched the movements of the actors' mouths onscreen. Walt thought that the same technology could be used to make a cartoon with sound. He worked on a new idea, and his team soon started preparing a Mickey Mouse cartoon called *Steamboat Willie*. About halfway through the process, Walt began to wonder if a cartoon with sound would be too silly. Would the audience think that it was strange to have cartoon making sounds? Would this be the biggest mistake of his career so far?

Walt decided to take some Disney employees and their wives and put on a special preview of

Steamboat Willie for them. A projector was set up outside a window (so that the noise wouldn't distract the audience), and a group of Disney employees, including Walt, got together in a room next door and made the music, sound effects, and spoken words for the cartoon. They listened to a steady ticking sound to know when they needed to make each sound. How did the audience react? Walt later said:

> "The effect on our little audience was nothing less an electric. They responded almost instinctively to this union of sound and motion. I thought they were kidding me. So they put me in the audience and ran the action again. It was terrible, but it was wonderful! And it was something new!"

His friend and chief animator Ubbe Iwerks later said:

"I've never been so thrilled in my life. Nothing since has ever equaled it".[8]

Once he and his team had finished the cartoon entirely in 1928, they found a distributor who gave them the equipment they needed to get this new cartoon (with sound) into theaters across the country.

The entire nation loved the new cartoon. They loved the sound, they loved the music, and they loved Mickey Mouse. He was funny, lovable, and most importantly to Walt – he was watchable. For almost twenty years, Walt himself provided the voice for Mickey Mouse. It was later said that Ubbe Iwerks gave Mickey his body, but Walt gave him his personality and soul.[9]

It wasn't long before Mickey Mouse was more popular than even Felix the Cat. Disney

---

[8]   Disney   and   Iwerks   quotes:
http://www.filmsound.org/animation/steamboatwilly/

[9] Idea: http://tinyurl.com/mr23hdw

produced toys and other merchandise (like plates and cups) with Mickey's face all over them - and the world couldn't get enough. In fact, during the next decade, audiences in many different countries would fall in love with Mickey, Minnie, Donald Duck, Goofy, Pluto, and the whole gang of Disney characters that Walt and his team eventually created.

After he saw what a hit *Steamboat Willie* had been, Walt wanted to create a new series of cartoons based around sound. He called them *Silly Symphonies*. In 1932, Walt decided that sound wasn't enough. He was going to take the technology of cartoon animation another step forward – he added color to a *Silly Symphonies* cartoon (called *Flowers and Trees*). It was so popular and well done that Walt won an Academy Award for it. By 1935, Mickey Mouse himself had been redesigned and drawn in color, making him even more popular than Popeye.

The whole world was taking notice of this amazing man, Walt Disney, and his imagination. To add to his happiness, in 1933 Lillian Disney gave birth to a daughter they named Diane, and in 1936, the Disneys adopted a baby girl named Sharon.

However, Walt's life wasn't without problems. His longtime animator Ubbe Iwerks left him in 1930 to work on his own series, and it he wouldn't work again with Disney until ten years had passed.

By 1934, Walt Disney was enjoying a lot of success. He had started two popular series of cartoons (Mickey Mouse and *Silly Symphonies*) and had won a prestigious Academy Award for his work. While he was making quite a bit of money with his short cartoons, but Walt imagined that cartoons could still be better. He imagined a world where entire feature length films would be animated, telling compelling stories and introducing characters that would get the audience emotionally involved.

When Walt told some of the people that he worked with about his idea to make a feature-length animated film, a lot of them thought it was a bad idea. Even his brother and business partner Roy and his wife Lillian tried to get Walt to change his mind. But Walt trusted that his ideas were good and that his imagination could make anything possible. So in 1934 he and his team started working on *Snow White and the Seven Dwarves*.

Critics of Disney at the time said that making the film would be Walt's biggest mistake, and even called it "Disney's Folly". They were sure that no one would want to sit for over one hour watching cartoon characters on the big screen. They thought that no one would take the story seriously, and some folks even thought that watching cartoons for too long would give the audience a headache.

Although part of his team kept making Mickey Mouse and *Silly Symphony* cartoons, a large number of animators worked hard to make the most realistic looking animation possible to tell the story of Snow White. Behind the scenes, Walt and his team also worked hard to create serious dialogue and believable characters that wouldn't distract the audience from the beautiful love story they were trying to tell.

Along with character development, Disney decided to try some new technology to make this film seem even more realistic. Instead of just taking pictures of one drawing at a time, as most animators did, some of Walt's engineers developed a special camera called a multiplane camera. This special camera could take pictures of up to eight pictures at a time, one stacked on top of another. The advantage of this camera was that it made movement look more realistic and made the scenery seem almost real enough to touch. Tested out in a *Silly Symphonies* cartoon, this camera was used quite a bit in *Snow White and the Seven Dwarves* and in later Disney films (like *Bambi*).

By late 1937, the film was close to being finished - but because the cost of making the movie was so high (over $250,000) - Walt realized that his studio would soon run out of money. To be able to finish his revolutionary *Snow White* project, he had to convince some people to loan him more money. How could Walt convince these professional bankers to support what everyone else was calling a mistake? Simple – he showed them the parts of the film that he had finished so far.

The bankers were so impressed with what they saw of the film that they gave Disney the money he needed to finish it. On December 21, 1937, the film was shown for the first time to the public. How did they react? Did they react to the film like Disney wanted them to or did they think it was a silly waste of time?

10

Audiences loved *Snow White*. They laughed at the jokes, they were delighted by the songs, and they even cried as Snow White was laid in her glass coffin after eating the poison apple. The movie eventually made over $8 million, making it the highest earning movie of the year, and for a brief time one of the highest earning sound pictures of all time. In fact, if you adjust for inflation (which describes the way that money changes value over time) *Snow White and the*

10   Image:
http://en.wikipedia.org/wiki/File:Walt_Disney_Snow_white_1937_
trailer_screenshot_(13).jpg

Seven Dwarves is the tenth highest earning movie of all time.

Suddenly, what everyone had been calling Walt Disney's greatest mistake turned out to be one of his biggest successes. After paying back his loans, Walt started production on a series of feature-length films, including *Pinocchio* and *Fantasia*. This period was known as "The Golden Age of Animation", a time when Walt and his team worked shoulder to shoulder like a family.

With a few exceptions, the years after *Snow White* came out were some of the happiest of Walt's life. His business was doing well, he felt challenged and satisfied at his job, and his family was growing. But in 1938, shortly after Walt finished *Snow White*, tragedy struck.

Walt and Roy Disney's mother, Flora, died from a gas leak in the house that her sons had bought for her. The boys had tried to do something pleasant for their parents and had never expected something like that to happen. Walt was crushed, and his father never quite got over the tragedy.

To cope with the pain, Walt threw himself into his work.

But Walt Disney's studio began to have some problems a few years after *Snow* White came out. Some factors beyond his control changed the world of entertainment.

In 1939, German Chancellor Adolf Hitler invaded nearby Poland and started World War Two. With cities and countries being invaded in Europe, suddenly no one could afford to watch Disney films overseas. Walt lost about 40% of his audience because of the war, and that meant that Walt's latest films (*Pinocchio* and *Fantasia*) did not end up making as much money as he had hoped they would.

It was around this time that Walt decided to make some changes in his studio – starting with the way he paid his animators. Instead of splitting the profits that each project made with them, he decided to pay his animators bonuses based on whether or not he thought that they had done exceptional work. Some of the animators felt that they weren't being paid fairly for their hard work, so, in 1941, they decided to go on strike.

The strike came when the team was working on *Dumbo* and lasted for about five weeks. A lot of newspapers talked about what was going on, and Walt felt like he had been betrayed by members of his own family. Because there was so much arguing going on, a friend of Walt's in the US government suggested that Walt go spend some time in South America while things cooled off in California.

Walt could take a sort of goodwill tour and strengthening American friendships with foreign countries. In fact, Walt even got to make some movies with what he learned there, including *Saludos Amigos* and *The Three Caballeros*.

By the time Walt got back from his trip, a lot had changed. Sadly, his father had died before Walt could say goodbye to him, and that made him sad. But peace had been made between the animators and the studio, and the strikers had gotten busy working again. Disney agreed to let his animators be a part of the animator's union, and everyone was happy to stop fighting and to start drawing again.

By the end of the 1940s, Walt Disney and his team were recovering from the financial problems of the war and were excited to start making more feature length films. They worked on *Bambi, Cinderella, Peter Pan* and *Alice in Wonderland*, and even made several live action nature films.

But perhaps one of the most important events of the 1940s came one afternoon when Walt Disney was watching his daughters play at a local park. He looked around and saw all the parents sitting on benches, just watching while the children had fun on the swings and slides. He thought: 'Wouldn't it be nice to have a park where parents and children could have fun together?'

Walt liked the idea so much that he decided to start talking about it with his team. At first he just wanted to build a special park that people visiting Disney studios could experience. The attractions would be based on some of the films and TV shows that Disney and his team had worked on. But Walt's ideas were too large for a small park, especially because he wanted visitors from all over the world to be able to be a part of the magic that he had in mind.

By the late 1940s, Walt Disney had entertained people for decades with his cartoon films. But now he had an even bigger idea: he would build a theme park, and he would call it "Disneyland".

It would be the happiest place on Earth.

Chapter 4: Later Life

The first challenge of designing his new theme park was to find a place large enough to build it. Walt had originally thought of using a piece of land near his studio in Burbank, but with all of the ideas that his imagination was coming up with, it was soon clear that more space would be needed. So Walt sent out a team of employees to find a large piece of land with highway access (so people could find it easily) and with enough space to build everything that they had in mind.

Within a short time, Walt's team found a 160-acre orange and walnut grove in the small town of Anaheim. The land looked like it just might work. Work began on Disneyland in 1954, and by 1955, the project had been completed. For this park, there would be no one to tell Walt what he could and could not do. This park would be entirely the product of Walt Disney's imagination, and everything in it would be just the way he wanted it to be.

For starters, Walt would keep his park clean, unlike the Electric Park in Kansas City that Walt and his sister Ruth visited as a kid. And Walt was sure to include one of the most important things from his childhood: a large steam-powered train. When planning the park, Walt had told his team: "I just want it to look like nothing else in the world. And it should be surrounded by a train."[11]

Walt decided to divide the park into five lands. The first was called Main Street, USA, and had shops, a cinema, a railroad, and a fire engine, just like small towns around the turn of the century used to have. Walt's childhood town of Marceline, Missouri, was a tremendous influence on him when he designed Main Street, USA.

---

[11] Quote: http://www.quoteswise.com/walt-disney-quotes-6.html

Main Street, USA would take visitors straight to a castle that looked like it was from a fairy tale.

12

The other four lands were Adventureland, Frontierland, Fantasyland, and Tomorrowland. Because Walt was already known for having produced both cartoons and live action films, he made sure to include a little bit of everything in the lands. He built rides and adventures based on the films and TV shows *20,000 Leagues under the Sea*, *Davy Crockett- King of the Wild Frontier*, *Dumbo*, *Peter Pan*, and *Snow White and the Seven Dwarves*. He designed rides to

12 Image: http://www.designingdisney.com/content/construction-disneyland

take his guests on trips to see wild animals in the jungle, and entertained them with Wild West saloon shows. Kids could fly into the air like Dumbo and drive cars on the Autotopia. Families could ride a steamboat named after Mark Twain and could even travel to the moon on a rocket.

These rides and attractions let the audience feel like they were a part of their favorite movie or TV show. Some rides were outdoors, some were indoors. But no matter how they were built each one transported its passengers to a faraway place.

Disneyland itself was surrounded by high walls and trees so that everyone who walked through the main gates could forget that they were in Southern California and could imagine that they were in a magical land where everything that they had seen on the big screen was coming to life all around them. Their favorite characters, including Mickey, Minnie, and Donald Duck, would walk the streets and interact with the guests.

On July 17, 1955, Disneyland officially opened to the public. As we saw in the introduction, there were quite a few problems on opening day. Too many people showed up, there wasn't enough food or water for the people who wanted it, and the soft asphalt made walking kind of uncomfortable for some of the attendees.

Some critics said that the park opening was a disaster and that it would ruin Disney - but soon enough those same critics began to change their minds. Walt invited many of them back to his park a short while later to see Disneyland as it was meant to be, and everyone was hugely impressed. And just as Walt had wanted, parents and kids were everywhere, spending time together and having fun together in his park.

Walt once said about the place that he had helped to create:

> "Disneyland will never be completed. It will continue to grow as long as there is imagination left in the world. It is something that will never be finished. Something that I can keep developing and adding to."[13]

Even during his lifetime, Walt tried to make sure that his park was bigger and better each, and every time that guests came to visit it. He saw to it that there were new attractions to keep repeat visitors entertained, and also made sure that older attractions were well taken care of so that they would last from one generation to the next.

In the early 1950s, before Disneyland had become a reality, Walt had brought home a souvenir from a vacation that he took. It was a

---

[13] Quote: http://tinyurl.com/jvodut2

small mechanical bird that could move its body. The bird inspired Walt, and he began thinking how delightful it would be to use technology to give lots of different kinds of 3D figures lives and personality, just as he had done with his cartoon animations. Some members of Walt's team began to work on 3D models, and in 1964 Walt Disney officially announced the existence of "audio-animatronics". This was the term he used to describe his team's methods of making 3D figures come to life.

Disneyland was already a considerable success by the 1960s, but as part of his quest to make the park ever bigger and better Walt thought that he should use more audio-animatronics technology. So in 1963 he opened a new attraction using audio-animatronic figures and a pre-recorded soundtrack. He called it The Enchanted Tiki Room.

The Enchanted Tiki Room was a colossal hit right away. Set in the tropical South Seas, the room had over 150 moving figures - mostly birds and talking statues - that sang a song and put on a show for the audience. The figures moved perfectly in time with the music, talked with the audience and made them laugh. The technology worked just as Walt had hoped it would. It gave the figures life and distinct personalities. People loved the attraction, so in 1964 Walt showed off his audio-animatronic technology at the World's

---

14 Image: http://thedisneydrivenlife.com/2011/08/26/walt-disneys-enchanted-tiki-room/

Fair in New York, using an animated figure of President Abraham Lincoln giving a speech.

Disney thought that films might be better with audio-animatronics, and so in the 1964 film *Mary Poppins* he included two audio-animatronic birds. Soon after the movie came out, Walt started overseeing the construction of a ride being built at Disneyland (in a new section called New Orleans Square). The ride would called Pirates of the Caribbean and would use lots of full sized audio-animatronic figures to tell a scary story about pirates attacking a coastal village and stealing its treasure.

Around this same time that Walt and his brother Roy began to design an even larger theme park in Florida, which would be called Disneyworld.

Unfortunately, Walt Disney would not get to see the finished versions of either the Pirates ride or the Disneyworld project. He died unexpectedly of heart failure on December 15, 1966, at the age of 65.

Walt Disney had been a heavy smoker his whole life (although he tried to make sure that his younger fans never saw him smoking). A polo player in his younger days, Walt had suffered a neck injury a long time ago and needed to get a surgery. While getting ready for the operation, doctors took an X-ray of Walt's chest and saw that he had a cancerous tumor in his left lung.

Doctors removed Walt's lung in November of 1966 to try and save him, but a few weeks later he collapsed in his house. Doctors did their best to keep this great man alive, but he was too sick and died in the hospital just two weeks later.

The final films that he directly helped to make were *The Jungle Book* and *The Happiest Millionaire*.

After he died, some people started to tell kind of strange stories about Walt Disney, even saying that his body was kept frozen somewhere in

Disneyland and that he might come back to life at any moment. While Walt Disney certainly had an incredible imagination (and lots of money) his daughter said that the rumors weren't true at all and that her father was cremated and buried like most other people at the time were.

Walt Disney's death was terribly sad, but soon after he died something amazing happened – the parks and the films that he had helped to create kept on entertaining audiences worldwide. New rides were added, new animations were released, and new technology was put to good use. After a little while, it was clear that Walt Disney had built something much bigger than himself – he had built a legacy that would continue on long after he died.

Although his unique imagination wasn't around anymore, the characters that Walt Disney had created, and the view of the world that he had promoted would keep on living.

Chapter 5: Why Walt Disney Was Important

Walt Disney was a man who let his imagination influence his life and work. From the time that he was a child in Missouri, standing outside the Electric Park and sketching pictures of his neighbor's horse, his imagination moved him to think of the world as a different place from what it was. Walt imagined how things could be, and then worked his hardest to make those visions a reality.

There were moments in his life when the people around Walt didn't share his ideas or enthusiasm. When he wanted to make a cartoon with sound, he doubted himself. When he wanted to make a feature-length animated film, his family and friends told him that it would be a mistake. And when he wanted to open a theme park, critics said that it would ruin him. But through it all Walt Disney pushed forward, sure that his imagination could make his dreams come true and would make the world a better place.

Today, almost 16 million people a year visit Disneyland. There are also parks in Florida, Japan, China, and France that draw millions more visitors each and every year. And the company founded by Walt, called the Walt Disney Company, continues to play an important role in inspiring everyone who comes into contact with it, both young and old.

Just as Walt would have wanted, Disneyland has continued to grow and adapt to changes throughout the years. As guests started to show more interest in fast rides, Disneyland built a bobsled ride on the Matterhorn, a log ride called Splash Mountain, the Big Thunder Mountain Railroad, and a science-fiction experience called Space Mountain. 3D movies were shown in a

Tomorrowland theater, and partnerships with director George Lucas led to two new attractions: *Star Tours* and *The Indiana Jones Adventure*.

With each new generation of visitors to Disney parks, something is created just for them. But the connection to the past has not been lost in all the innovation. In fact, Disneyland still has 14 of its original attractions that today's guests can experience (including the popular spinning teacups). Everywhere that guests go in the park, they are reminded of the imaginative man who made it all possible.

The Walt Disney Corporation has also been able to serve as a preserving influence for many entertainment families. For example, there are some characters may have disappeared entirely if it weren't for Disney stepping in to buy them and preserve them. The Muppets were bought by Disney in 2004, and Oswald the Lucky Rabbit was bought back by Disney in 2006. Pixar was also purchased in 2006, making sure that the characters of *Toy Story*, *Cars*, and *Finding Nemo* would have a safe home for the future. In 2009, characters from the Marvel universe were purchased, and the *Star Wars* franchise was bought in 2012.

In a time of problems brought on by the Great Depression and World War Two, Walt Disney helped people to forget about their troubles and to believe in something magic. In a time where families didn't spend as much together as they should, Walt Disney made a place for parents to laugh alongside their kids and to have adventures together. In a time when science had answered some of life's greatest questions, Walt Disney has shown us that there are still a lot of things out there that we don't understand and that there is still a lot of wonder left in the world.

Walt Disney has inspired the next generation of thinkers to use their imaginations. Even after all of the films he produced and loveable characters he created, perhaps that is his legacy.

Walt Disney's greatest gift to the world was his imagination.

15

---

[15] Image: http://thewaltdisneycompany.com/about-disney/disney-history/1960-01-01--1969-12-31

29346625R00039

Made in the USA
Middletown, DE
16 February 2016